MOUNTAIN RANGES
OF THE WORLD

Andes, Rockies, Himalayas, Atlas, Alps

Introduction to Geography Grade 4 | Children's Science & Nature Books

BABY PROFESSOR
EDUCATION KIDS

First Edition, 2020

Published in the United States by Speedy Publishing LLC, 40 E Main Street, Newark, Delaware 19711 USA.

Baby Professor Books are available at special discounts when purchased in bulk for industrial and sales-promotional use. For details contact our Special Sales Team at Speedy Publishing LLC, 40 E Main Street, Newark, Delaware 19711 USA. Telephone (888) 248-4521 Fax: (210) 519-4043. www.speedybookstore.com

10 9 8 7 6 * 5 4 3 2 1

Print Edition: 9781541959828
Digital Edition: 9781541962828

See the world in pictures. Build your knowledge in style.
www.speedypublishing.com

TABLE OF CONTENTS

Although water covers around seventy percent of the Earth, there are different types of landforms as well. A mountain is an example of one such landform. This book will define what a mountain is, briefly tell how different types of mountains may be formed and highlight the features of five different mountain ranges.

High detailed image of Earth

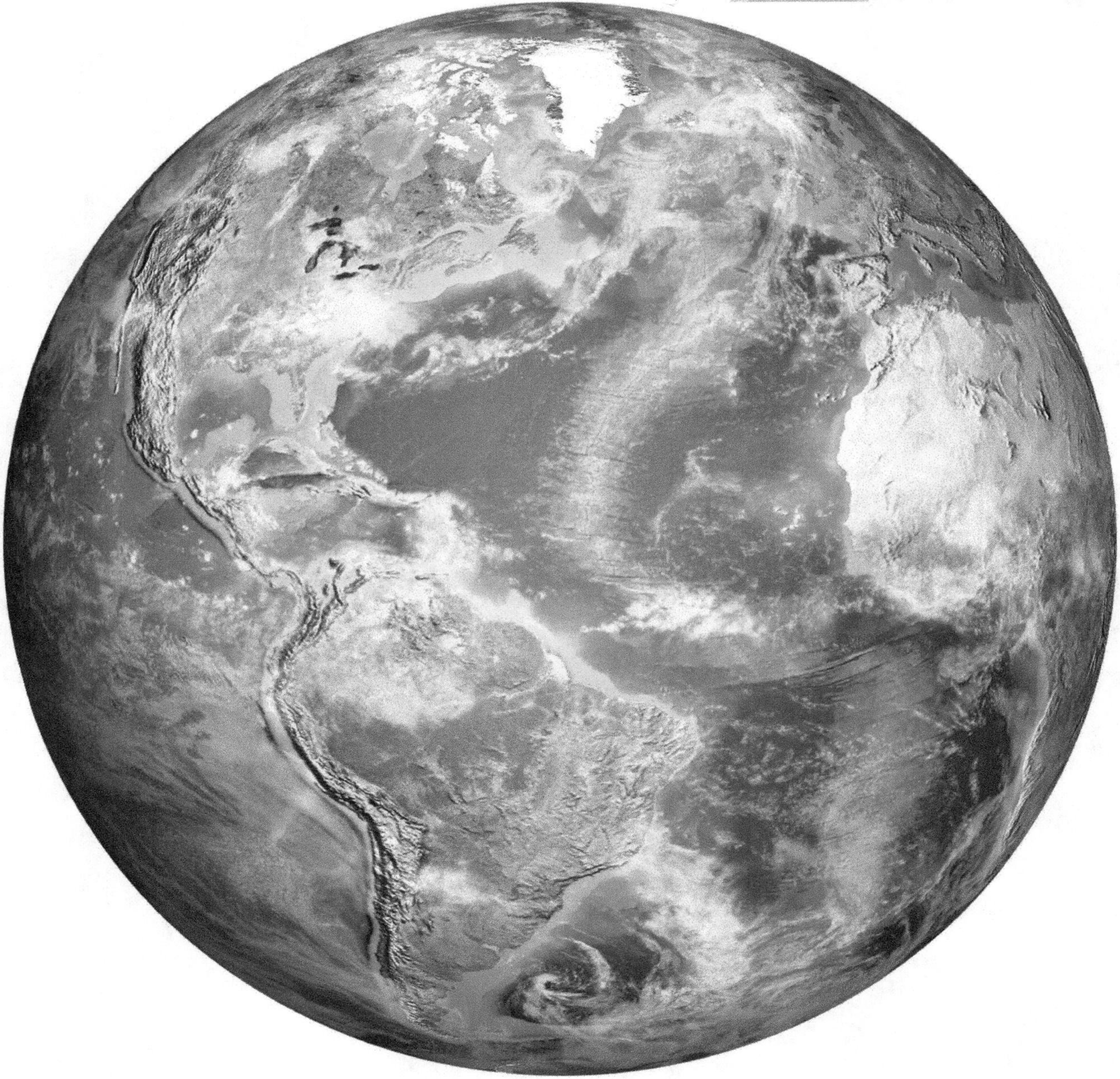

WHAT IS A MOUNTAIN AND HOW IS
IT FORMED?

A mountain is a very tall landform that is much higher than any other piece of land. A mountain is not to be confused with a hill. A mountain is much taller than a hill and it is has certain features that distinguish it from a hill.

Mountains in the southern region of Iceland.

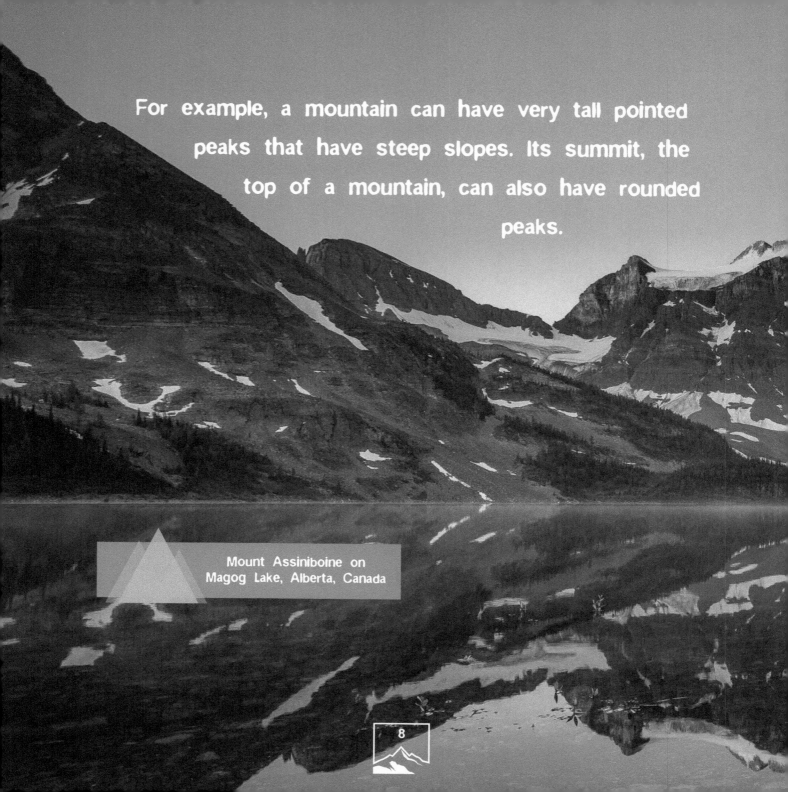

For example, a mountain can have very tall pointed peaks that have steep slopes. Its summit, the top of a mountain, can also have rounded peaks.

Mount Assiniboine on Magog Lake, Alberta, Canada

Moreover, it is common to see a group of mountains together in the same area and this is known as a mountain range.

It is believed that mountains form in a couple different ways. One way is through the theory of tectonic plates. The surface of the Earth, which is called the crust, is made up of enormous pieces or plates of rock that move at an incredibly slow rate. Over a period, these plates bang into each other. When this happens, rock and land have no choice but to be shifted upward. The result is a mountain.

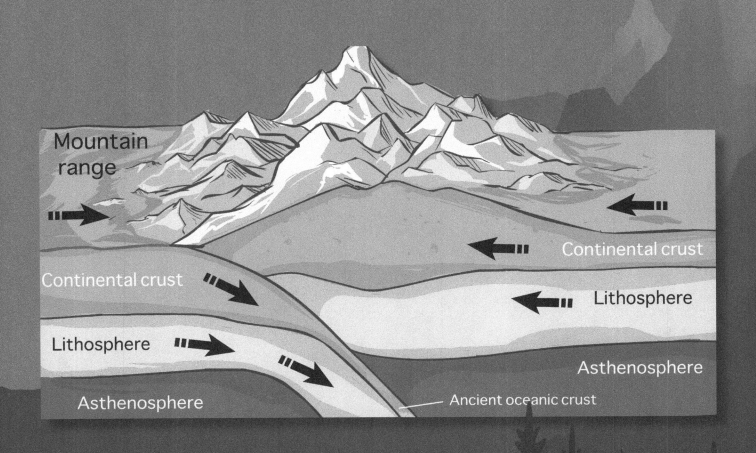

Mountain range

Continental crust

Continental crust

Lithosphere

Lithosphere

Asthenosphere

Asthenosphere

Ancient oceanic crust

An illustration of how mountains form through the theory of plate tectonics

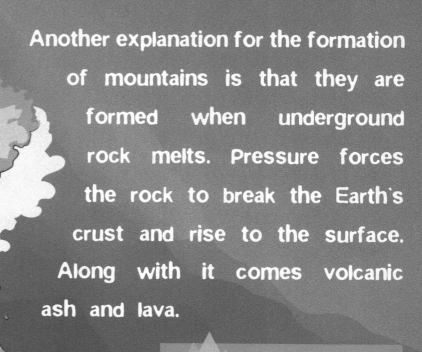

Another explanation for the formation of mountains is that they are formed when underground rock melts. Pressure forces the rock to break the Earth's crust and rise to the surface. Along with it comes volcanic ash and lava.

Formation of a volcanic mountain

This type of mountain formation is known as a volcanic mountain.

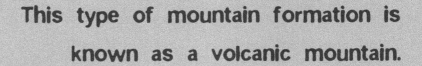

Stratovolcano Bolshaya Udina Volcano, Kamchatka Peninsula, Eurasia

FIVE DIFFERENT MOUNTAIN
RANGES ON EARTH:
THE ANDES

The Andes Mountains, the longest mountain range on Earth, are found in South America. Occupying an area on the west of South America, they extend all the way from the north to the tip of the south.

The Andes Mountains,
Argentina Chile

15

A South America map showing the location of the Andes Mountains.

They are so close to the Pacific Ocean that they are only separated from it by a narrow strip of land. Additionally, they are the highest range of mountains in both North and South America.

The highest peak, Mount Aconcagua in the country of Argentina, reaches a height of 22,831 feet.

Mount Aconcagua in Mendoza, Argentina

17

The Andes Mountains contain many fascinating land features. The Earth's largest river, the Amazon River, is found there.

Amazon rainforest river

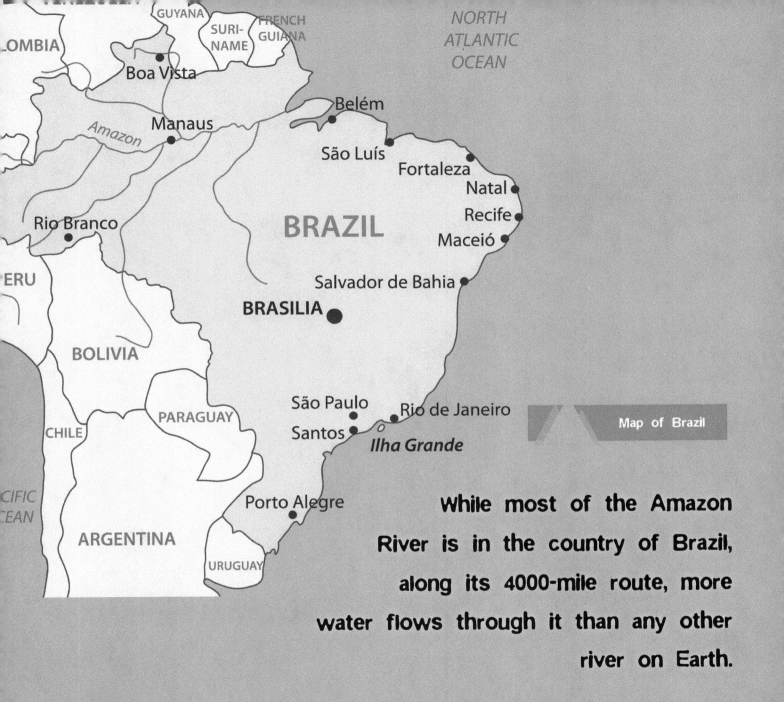

GUYANA
SURI-NAME
FRENCH GUIANA

NORTH
ATLANTIC
OCEAN

COLOMBIA

Boa Vista

Amazon

Manaus

Belém

São Luís

Fortaleza

Natal

Recife

BRAZIL

Maceió

Rio Branco

PERU

Salvador de Bahia

BRASILIA

BOLIVIA

São Paulo

Rio de Janeiro

PARAGUAY

Santos

Ilha Grande

CHILE

Map of Brazil

PACIFIC OCEAN

Porto Alegre

ARGENTINA

URUGUAY

While most of the Amazon River is in the country of Brazil, along its 4000-mile route, more water flows through it than any other river on Earth.

19

Many different types of minerals, volcanoes and glaciers, big sheets of ice, can be found in the Andes Mountains. Lower levels of the mountain range are home to beautiful tropical forests.

The Monte Fitz Roy is a mountain located in Patagonia, in the Andes Mountain range.

Andean condor, the largest flying bird in the world

High above its peaks, the Andean condor, a very big vulture, can be seen flying.

Colombian natural regions

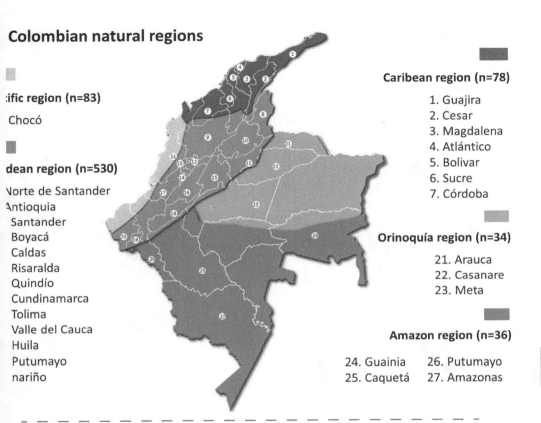

ific region (n=83)

Chocó

dean region (n=530)

Norte de Santander
Antioquia
Santander
Boyacá
Caldas
Risaralda
Quindío
Cundinamarca
Tolima
Valle del Cauca
Huila
Putumayo
nariño

Caribean region (n=78)

1. Guajira
2. Cesar
3. Magdalena
4. Atlántico
5. Bolivar
6. Sucre
7. Córdoba

Orinoquía region (n=34)

21. Arauca
22. Casanare
23. Meta

Amazon region (n=36)

24. Guainia   26. Putumayo
25. Caquetá   27. Amazonas

Map of Andean Region

b) Andean Sub-region

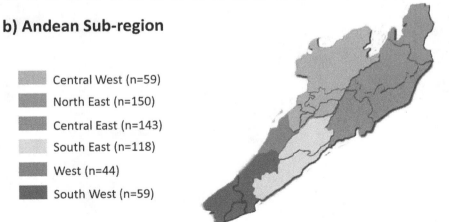

Central West (n=59)
North East (n=150)
Central East (n=143)
South East (n=118)
West (n=44)
South West (n=59)

The Andean region has been inhabited for approximately 10,000 years, with the first people being Indigenous Indians.

The Inca were a group of people who formed a civilization in the region. While today most people who inhabit the Andean region are farmers, mineral mining has also become common.

Inca people formed a civilization in the region

THE ROCKIES

The Rockies is a nickname for
the Rocky Mountains.

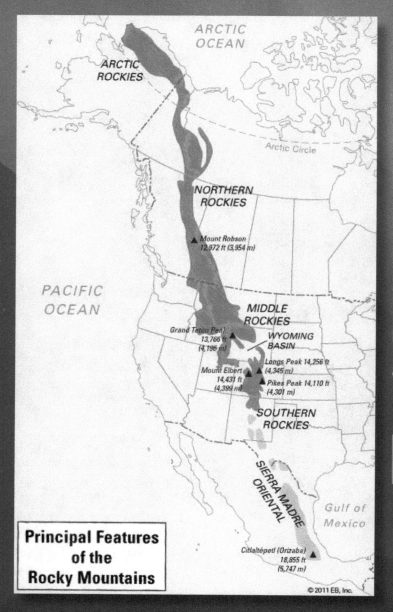

ARCTIC
OCEAN

ARCTIC
ROCKIES

Arctic Circle

NORTHERN
ROCKIES

PACIFIC
OCEAN

Mount Robson
12,972 ft (3,954 m)

MIDDLE
ROCKIES

Grand Teton Peak
13,766 ft
(4,196 m)

WYOMING
BASIN

Longs Peak 14,256 ft
(4,345 m)

Mount Elbert
14,431 ft
(4,399 m)

Pikes Peak 14,110 ft
(4,301 m)

SOUTHERN
ROCKIES

SIERRA MADRE
ORIENTAL

Gulf of
Mexico

Citlaltépetl (Orizaba)
18,855 ft
(5,747 m)

**Principal Features
of the
Rocky Mountains**

© 2011 EB, Inc.

This mountain range is found in the western area of North America. It is a very big mountain range that occupies space in parts of Canada as well as the United States.

A map showing the location of the Rockies.

28

The Rocky Mountains are sometimes considered to start in Alaska because they join a mountain range there.

Rocky mountain range in Glacier Bay Alaska

Then, they extend through northwest Canada and go all the way down to New Mexico.

Moraine Lake in Banff National Park, Canadian Rockies

They span a total surface area of 3000 miles in length and at their most narrow part, they measure 300 miles in width.

Rocky Mountain National
Park Estes Park
Colorado

31

At its highest peak, which is Mount Elbert, it is 14,433 feet tall and this peak is found in Colorado.

Mount Elbert, Colorado

The Rocky Mountains were first inhabited by Indigenous North Americans over 12,000 years ago.

Cherokee Trail, Colorado, from a sketch made in June of 1859

33

Today, many people like to explore the Rocky Mountains as tourists because of the breathtaking scenery. Different sections have been turned into parks.

Rocky Mountains,
Kananaskis Country
Alberta Canada

34

People can enjoy nature in many ways there, a couple of which are mountain climbing and skiing.

Rocky Mountains National Park, Colorado

Because the Rocky Mountains occupy such a vast area, different trees, lakes, minerals, oil, coal and natural gas can be found there.

Aspen, Colorado silver mining in 1898

Many of the mountains are capped with snow and there are different lakes.

Bear Lake, Rocky Mountains, Colorado

A variety of trees such as Douglas fir, aspen, western red cedar, western hemlock and white pine grow in the forests along this mountain range.

Douglas Fir

Aspen

Western red cedar

Western hemlock

White pine

In addition to the trees, certain animals live in the Rocky Mountains. In the northern region, a species from the big-horn family of sheep, the Rocky Mountain Sheep, can withstand the cold climate high up in the mountains. They can also navigate the ragged edges of rock without difficulty.

Big Horn Sheep

Other animals that make their home in the Rocky Mountains are grizzly bears, mountain lions, reindeer, mountain goats and elk. Large birds such as different types of eagles and falcons can be seen soaring above these mountains.

Grizzly bear

Mountain lion

Reindeer

Mountain goat

Elk

THE HIMALAYAS

The Himalayas or Himalayan Mountains, which translated from Indian Sanskrit means house or abode of snow, occupies different countries in Asia. It received this name because of the snow that is on the mountain tops.

Himalayan mountain, Uttarakhand near Badrinath, India

The mountain range extends across a west to east area of approximately 1550 miles in the countries of India, Nepal, the Tibet Autonomous Region of China and Bhutan.

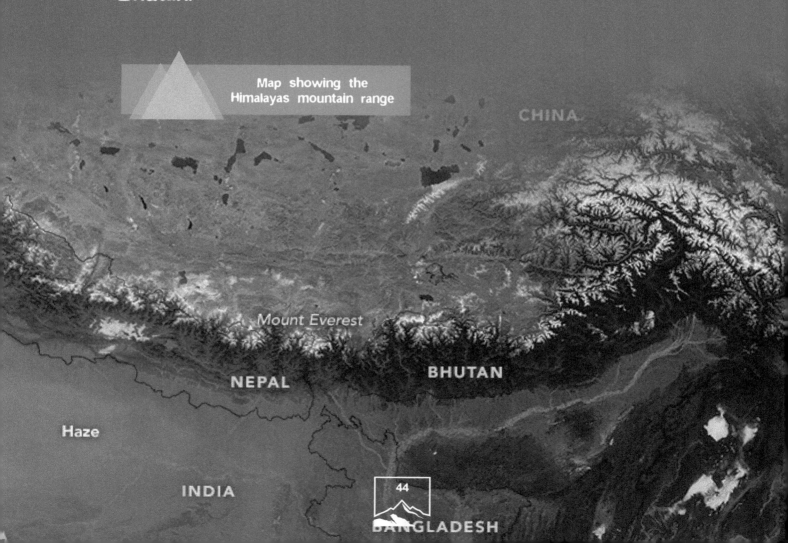

Map showing the Himalayas mountain range

The highest mountain on Earth, Mount Everest, which is 29,035 feet tall, is found in the Himalayan mountain range. Other very high mountain peaks are also found in this region.

Mount Everest, Nepal

In addition to the high peaks, nineteen rivers flow through the area. One of them, the Ganges River, is of great importance to India. Beginning in a cave filled with ice, it flows for about 1500 miles.

Ganges river, Rishikesh, India

Another well-known river is the Indus River, from which the country India gets its name.

Indus rivers, Ladakh, India

Although the weather conditions are inhospitable in the highest parts of the mountains, the lower levels are inhabited. The people who live there are of mixed races. Many people make their living by farming the land.

Inhabited part of the Nepal Himalayas, lower Solukhumbu

49

Rice, millet, wheat, sugarcane, corn, pears, cherries, peaches, and apples are all grown there.

Rice fields in a small Indian village near the Himalayas

In the part of the Himalayan region in India, a lot of people grow tea. The well-known Darjeeling tea, for example, is grown there.

Tea plantations in Munnar, Kerala, India

Some people, such as the Sherpa, work as guides to assist people who visit the area to mountain climb.

A Sherpa, Himalaya
Nepalese Mountain Guide

Some climbers try to scale Mount Everest. This is a very challenging task and there are people who have either lost their lives or sustained injuries trying to do so.

Sherpa guides and trekkers trekking to Everest base camp

The first two people to have reached the summit were a Sherpa guide by the name of Tenzing Norgay who accompanied Edmund Hillary of New Zealand. They made this great accomplishment in 1953.

Edmund Hillary and
Tenzing Norgay

THE ATLAS

The Atlas Mountains stretch over three countries in the north of the continent of Africa: Tunisia, Algeria and Morocco.

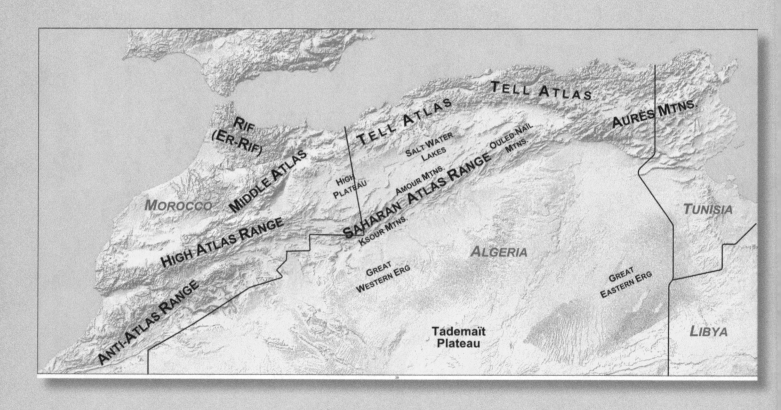

The Atlas mountain map

The
mountains
get their name
from Atlas, a
Greek mythological
figure whose
punishment was to
hold up the heavens in
the far west. This area is
associated with modern-day
northwest Africa.

Greek mythological
figure, Atlas

Several mountain ranges join to form what is known as the Atlas Mountains. The Atlas Mountains measure about 1200 miles in length.

The Atlas Mountains

59

Reaching a height of 13,664 feet, the highest peak is Toubkal. It is atop High Atlas in the country of Morocco.

60

Toubkal, the highest peak
of the Atlas Mountains

61

The Tell Atlas is the name given to the northern part of the Atlas Mountains. It is where cork oak trees, pine, green oak trees, heather, lavender and other vegetation can be found.

Trees and other vegetation in the Atlas Mountains

62

The Saharan Atlas refers to the region in the southern area. Because this area is much more arid than the north, fewer trees and vegetation grow there.

A part of the Anti-Atlas mountains seen from the south

To the east of the Atlas Mountains
is the Nile River, the longest river
on Earth. The Nile covers an area of
about 4132 miles.

Nile river on the east
of Atlas mountains

There are two groups of people who make parts of the Atlas Mountain their home. One group is the Berber people who dwell high up in the mountains.

Berber people traveling on camels

Most of them farm the land that is in the valleys below. Dates, figs, grapes and grains are grown in this area.

Dates

Figs

Grapes

Grains

The other group of people who inhabit the Atlas Mountain are Arabs. Many of the Arab people are nomadic, that is they move from place to place.

The Arabs in the Atlas mountains

Many of them are shepherds or goatherders. Although there used to be more animals in the Atlas Mountains, the animal population has declined.

An Arab goat herder

There are a few wild boar, monkeys and jackals left. Some minerals have also been found in the area.

Boar   Monkeys   Jackals

The three countries of Tunisia, Algeria and Morocco encourage tourism in the Atlas Mountains. Mining for minerals has also been done in the area.

A mining village deep in the Atlas mountains

THE ALPS

The Alps occupy many countries
in western Europe.

Swiss Alps, Europe

73

The countries are France, Italy, Switzerland, Liechtenstein, Germany, Austria, Albania, Montenegro, Bosnia and Herzegovina and Slovenia.

Alps Mountain Range

At 15,771 feet tall, the highest peak is Mount Blanc and it is in the country of France.

Mont Blanc Massif,
Alps, France

Farmland around
Alps mountain

The Alps have been inhabited for a very long time, between 50,000 and 60,000 years ago. The area around the Alps was used as farmland.

People still live in areas around the Alps and the population is dense.

Farmland in a European village, on the Alps mountains

Both trees and animals can be found in the Alps. Although the highest areas of the Alps do not contain many trees, at a certain altitude, pine, larch and spruce trees grow.

High areas of the Alps are bereft of trees.

At lower altitudes, other types of trees such as beech, chestnut and oak can be seen. Not many types of animals live in the Alps.

Different trees can be seen at the lower altitudes of the Alps.

Precipitation in the form of snow and rain is abundant in the Alps. A lot of ice is located on its peak.

The Alps from the Titlis Peak

Many of the areas in the valley contain glaciers. The Alps also experience a lot of avalanches, which can be very hazardous.

Austrian Alps

An avalanche is when a vast amount of snow forcefully tumbles down a mountain.

Huge avalanche in the French Alps

85

Nonetheless, many people go to the Alps to participate in skiing or mountain climbing. Many well-known ski resorts such as Saint Moritz in Switzerland, for example, attract tourists.

St. Moritz is a ski resort in the Swiss Alps

The Alps also contain different bodies of water. One is the Rhine River, which is roughly 765 miles in length, and it is one of the most significant rivers in Europe. It has played an important part in the economy and history of several European countries.

Rhine river

There are also many different lakes in this Alpine region. Some of the more well-known include Lake Como, Lake Constance and Lake Geneva. All these lakes are surrounded by a spectacular scenery.

Lake Como

Lake Constance

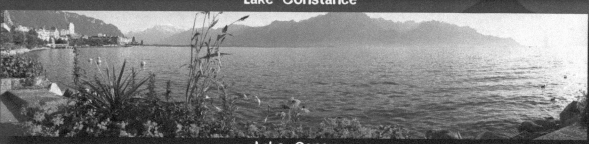
Lake Geneva

The Earth has different mountain ranges. Mountain ranges are a striking contrast to other landforms and oceans. While some are taller and longer than others, all of them have elements of awe and beauty.

An satellite image of Earth's landforms.

In addition to their awe and beauty, people rely on the areas around mountains as a place to live and to make a living.

A village near Alps mountains

90

Visit

BABY PROFESSOR
EDUCATION KIDS

www.speedypublishing.com

to download Free Baby Professor eBooks and view our
catalog of new and exciting Children's Books

CPSIA information can be obtained
at www.ICGtesting.com
Printed in the USA
BVHW062048280121
599006BV00005B/438